The Enneagram Personality Types

How to Use Your Personality to Evolve into the Best Version of Yourself and Have a Satisfying and Harmonic Life

Containing:

"Discover Yourself and Get the Most Out of Your Relationships"

"Embrace Your Potential and Overcome Your Weak Points"

by Eleanor Cooper

Table of Contents

Discover which Enneagram type are you!

I happily introduce you to the bonus content I've put together to give you along with this book. I used my knowledge on Enneagram and several real-life experiences to refine this **Enneagram Test** for you.

With this test, you will learn your type in just a few minutes, get it now.

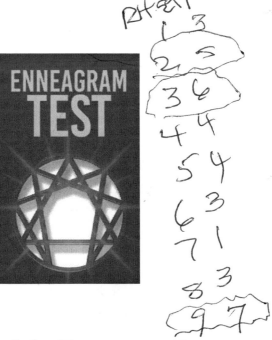

Download the Enneagram Test
by visiting this link:

http://eepurl.com/dtlgxf

ENNEAGRAM

------ ❧❦❧ ------

*Discover Yourself and Get the Most
Out of Your Relationships*

by Eleanor Cooper

Introduction

I would like to thank you for purchasing this book, Enneagram: Discover Yourself and Get the Most Out of Your Relationships.

Ignorance is bliss. Or is it? Is ignorance bliss when it comes to self-awareness? You cannot be blissfully ignorant of yourself. If you want to achieve your goals in life, you need to be aware of yourself. What you don't know about yourself not only harms you but can even hurt your relationships as well. Do you need some help to figure things out? Do you feel like you are stuck in a rut? If yes, then this is the perfect book for you.

What does "Enneagram" mean? No, it isn't a mathematical equation. It is an ancient system of personality types. An Enneagram helps to describe the different personality types of human beings with uncanny precision. It helps to define how unusual and weird human beings are. There are nine personality types according to the Enneagram. Each of these types comes with its own set of positive and negative traits. In this book, you will learn about each of these personality types and how each type interacts with others.

If you want to know more about yourself, about those around you, and about your relationships in life, then this is the right book for you. If you are aware of yourself, you tend to become aware of the situations you come across in life. The first step to improve yourself is to understand yourself. If you are ready, then we can get started now!

Thank you once again for choosing this book; happy reading!

Chapter One:
About Enneagram

An Enneagram isn't a new concept, and in fact, it has been around for a long time. It describes nine types of personalities. Believe it or not, all of us tend to fall into one of these nine categories. Easy peasy, isn't it? Yes, it is as simple as that. The roots of the Enneagram trace back to the Middle East, and it is a useful tool for understanding human behavior. Enneagram is a combination of two Greek words, *ennea* and *grammos*. Ennea means nine, and grammos implies movement or something that's written.

A nine-pointed polygon is used to depict the Enneagram. Somewhere back in the 1900s, Georgi I. Gurdjieff introduced the western civilization to the concept of the Enneagram. He made use of this method to differentiate between a person's essence and personality. Oscar Ichazo is known as the father of modern variety of the Enneagram that we use today. He wrote about it for the first time during the 1950s.

The Enneagram is a pseudo-scientific method to identify a human being's personality type. There are nine types of personalities, and each of these is connected to the Enneagram with the help of fixed points and lines. The relationships of each of these personality types develop based on a few fixed patterns. You might associate yourself with more than one personality type, but there is just one dominant personality a person can possess unless you believe that you have a multiple personality disorder!

Benefits

The most important benefit that the Enneagram provides is that it will help you to understand yourself. It will help you to understand your inner self. It will also help you to understand others. When you understand others, you can be more compassionate towards them. The Enneagram will help you to not just access, but even expand your emotional, mental, and spiritual intelligence. You will be aware of your automatic responses and defensive reactions towards situations in life. When you are aware of the manner in which you react, you can change your reactions. The only thing that you can fully control in your life is your reactions. The difference between success and failure is your reaction. The way you react can decide the course of your life. Thus, the Enneagram will improve your efficiency when you interact with others. Not just that, it will help you to build meaningful relationships. It will help you to live in the present and not the past or the future. Well, it all boils down to self-awareness. Being aware of yourself will help you to change your life for the better.

Personality Types

The Enneagram is all about the essence of a being. It describes nine basic models of human behavior, and each of these types has certain qualities, both good and bad. If you gain an insight into these personality types, it will help you to understand your behavior as well as the behaviors of those around you. Not just that, it opens the path for personal development. So, let us look at these nine personality types.

Type 1: The Perfectionist

As the name suggests, a Perfectionist wants absolute perfection in everything. Regardless of what it is, they want to excel at everything. Perfectionists are quite realistic, thorough, meticulous, and principled. They tend to be control freaks and demand that everything be perfect. Anything that isn't perfect will trigger a Perfectionist's OCD (not literally). They are well disciplined, dependable, and like order in their life. However, they are impatient, demanding, and they can be extremely critical of themselves and others. Phew, stop being a constant critic and give yourself a break!

Type 2: The Helper

Helpers always want to be liked. Of course, they are ready to help. People with this personality type are usually caring. They are helpful to the extent of being self-effacing. They also find it quite challenging to say no, and end up in situations that are easily avoidable. On the downside, they can be meddlesome, jealous, and even possessive. Yes, jealousy and possessiveness are two distinct traits, and neither is desirable. A helper's helpful nature can be their undoing.

Type 3: The Achiever

What do Achievers want? Achievers always aim for success and will obtain it with a lot of hard work. They are very energetic, optimistic, self-assured, and goal-oriented. It sounds like they are quite sorted in life, doesn't it? People with this personality type are efficient and decisive. However, they can be manipulative, calculating, and selfish. Because of these negative traits, they often ignore what others feel. Life is a race for them, and they want to come out on top.

Type 4: The Individualist

People with this personality type are emotional. They are quite instinctive but tend to experience lots of ups and downs in life. They don't appreciate routine and monotonous jobs. A 9-5 job is their real nightmare. This personality type can be slightly emotionally unbalanced, and they tend to exaggerate a lot.

Type 5: The Observer

Observers like to observe, learn, and are always analytical. They want to rationalize things and don't let their emotions get the best of them. Not just that, when compared to other personality traits, they are insightful. The disadvantages of being rational and analytical all the time is that they may seem cold and devoid of emotions.

Type 6: The Loyalist

Loyalists always need safety and security. People with this personality type have a great sense of responsibility and are always dependable. They are sticklers for rules. On the downside, they tend to be extremely suspicious and have the ability to predict disasters.

Type 7: The Optimist

The main traits that describe this personality type apart from optimistic are energetic and lively. Optimists might seem impulsive and shallow to others. They tend to forget the real world and live in their dreamland.

Type 8: The Leader

Leaders aren't born; they are made. This is technically true. However, some people possess leadership traits naturally, and they fall into this category. This personality type tends to be self-confident, independent, direct, and protective. Leaders aren't afraid of anything, and they will not shy away from conflict when needed. However, they can seem intimidating, selfish, and even vindictive.

Type 9: The Mediator

The ninth and final personality type is that of the Mediator. Mediators crave unity and harmony. They can look at a situation from a different perspective. They can see the pros and cons of any scenario. This personality type tends to be good at negotiations and is quite adaptable. On the downside, Mediators get distracted rather quickly and can seem indecisive. They have a hard time when it comes to prioritizing things in their life.

Enneagram Wings

The nine personality types mentioned above are the dominant personality types. Apart from this, there is something that's known as Enneagram wings. There are nine dominant personality types, and each class has a specific edge of the polygon. There is one number on either side that flanks each of the dominant figures.

For instance, the wings for One are Nine and Two. The wings for Two are One and Three. The Wings for Three are Two and Four. The Wings for Four are Three and Five. The Wings for Five are Four and Six. The Wings for Six are Five and Seven. The Wings for Seven are Six and Eight. The Wings for Eight are Seven and Nine. The Wings for Nine are Eight and One. When you see the Enneagram symbol, you can easily spot this pattern. The Enneagram helps you to understand yourself and your growth. Wings don't change any of our dominant personality traits. Instead, they add other characteristics. Wings also explain why two people who share the same style tend to behave differently.

Chapter Two:
Enneagram and Self-Discovery

The Enneagram personality type system is very dynamic and enlightening. We all tend to gravitate towards one of the dominant personality types. If you understand yourself, then you can begin to understand how your character traits affect your life. Once you know this, you can then make the necessary changes to achieve your goals in life. When you start to learn more about these nine personality types, you will begin to see specific patterns in which you have been living all this while. The first step is to explore each of these personality types so that you know the kind that suits you. In the journey towards self-discovery, the first step is awareness. When you become aware of your behavior, you can start to make changes consistently. So, let us learn a little more about all these personality types.

Type 1: The Perfectionist

Type One is known as the Perfectionist or the Reformer. Believe it or not, this personality type tends to be harder on themselves than anyone else around them. They often tend to be quite critical of themselves and their inner critic never takes a rest. At times, they can be wise and discerning. However, they are demanding and nit-picking. Type Ones often strive to achieve perfection that is somehow always out of their reach. They not only have high standards for themselves but others as well.

They want to do the right thing and are quite responsible; this makes them the ideal employee.

Not just that, they tend to have impossibly high moral standards. In fact, they are an excellent example of what integrity and ethics should look like. Well, the world of politics can certainly use more Ones.

They might strive for perfection, but this doesn't make them fearless. They fear to be wrong. The need to be right and to do good is quite an endearing trait of the Ones. At their best, they are rational, principled, idealistic, and productive. They are reform-minded and continuously think of ways in which they can improve themselves. They have the mindset of a perfectionist. They are quite orderly and emotionally constrained. At their worst, they are inflexible, extremely judgmental (of themselves and others alike), hypocritical, and even self-righteous. Ones believe that they are objective and reasonable, regardless of what others think of them.

Critical motivators for Ones include living up to their own high standards, excelling in everything that they do, and being efficient. They want to be fair in all their dealings, and they honestly want to make the world a better place to live in.

This personality type does sound too good to be true, doesn't it? The attributes that are favorable for them are also the ones that hinder their growth in life. It is quite likely that famous celebrities like Al Gore, Gandhi, Hillary Clinton, Jerry Brown, Margaret Thatcher, Joan Baez, Katherine Hepburn, Bill

Moyers, Martha Stewart, Thomas Jefferson, Ralph Nader, Sandra Day O'Connor, and Kenneth Starr are all Type One personalities.

My message to all the Ones out there is that you are okay if you do what you think is right. Having high standards for yourself and others is okay. However, you might not even realize that this attitude can cause you lots of problems. In fact, you can solve half of your troubles if you just cut yourself some slack. Give yourself a break, and give others a break. Everyone deserves it.

Type 2: The Helper

Type Two, or the Helpers, as their name suggests, are quite good at giving, but not so much at receiving. They are generous and always want to help others. There is a reason why they like to help others; it makes them feel like they are needed. They like to be required. People are drawn to all Twos like bees to honey because of their generous and helpful nature. They can do things for others without any expectations. They make excellent counselors. A person with this personality type can open up your heart because their heart is already open to the world. They can see the good in others.

There are three major things that all Twos believe. They believe that they should place the needs of others before their own. They should always give if they want to receive something. The third belief is that they must always work hard to earn the affection of others. These are the three beliefs that all the Twos firmly believe. In fact, these are the opinions they have held since their childhood. If you notice that you share these three beliefs, it is quite likely that you are a Two. Twos feel that it is selfish to have needs of their own. Well, that sounds kind of sad, doesn't it? The funny thing is, they aren't entirely selfless. They do have needs and expectations, but they are scared to acknowledge their needs. Melanie Hamilton from *Gone with the Wind* does seem like a perfect Type Two personality.

Their primary fear is that they are unloved or unwanted. They cannot stand the thought of not being loved by others. Since Twos like to feel needed, they never want to feel unwanted. They have an intense desire to feel loved. At their best, Twos are quite empathetic, concerned, nurturing, and loving. At their worst, Twos are quite possessive and manipulating. Their domineering nature can be quite a turn-off. They might not even realize that they are manipulative or any such thing. They believe that they are caring and loving people and they are, up to a certain extent.

The key motivating factors for Twos are that they want to give and receive unconditional love. The thought of being loved and accepted motivates them to do better. Famous personalities like Eleanor Roosevelt, Barbara Bush, Bishop Desmond Tutu, Albert Schweitzer, Leo Buscaglia, Jr., Ann Landers, Sammy Davis, Nancy Reagan, John Denver, Dolly Parton, Florence Nightingale, and Luciano Pavarotti are likely number Twos.

My message to all the Twos out there is that it is okay to let others love you. You don't always have to do something to feel loved. It is okay to receive even without giving at times. Learn to be a gracious receiver. You must understand the difference between loving and needing. Love and need are different; the sooner you know the difference, the more liberated you will feel. Having expectations is okay. In fact, you should acknowledge your expectations. No one is a mind reader, and at times you will have to spell out what you want from people. It doesn't make you selfish or shallow. So please stop thinking that.

Type 3: The Achiever

Type Three consists of all the go-getters and performers. They like to develop themselves and others around them. In comparison to other personality types, Type Threes get immense pleasure when they attain their goals. They are often successful and can motivate themselves to achieve their goals. The personal definition of success for Threes depends on their family lives, culture, and their social values. For some, a large home can signify success, for others it might be a good education, so on and so forth. Regardless of their definition of success, Threes want their family and community to view them as a success. Threes are therefore almost always goal-oriented in life. They often behave in a manner that will help them get the attention and praise they crave. In their childhood, Threes spend a lot of their time and energy on activities that are of value to their family members and peers. Their quotient of self-worth depends on other's definition of success. Without success, they will feel quite empty. Do you remember Don

Dapper from *Mad Men*? He is the embodiment of a type Three personality.

The primary fear of all the Threes is a feeling of worthlessness. They dread to think of their lives without the success that they hold dear to their heart. Their primary desire is to feel worthy and valuable. They are authentic, self-assured, motivated, and focused at their best. At their absolute worst, they can be quite pretentious, calculating, and even deceptive. They like to achieve success; the means don't always matter. They want to believe that they are outstanding. However, it is wrong when they think that they will be successful only if others believe that they are successful.

The key motivators for Threes are the goals they set for themselves. They want to become visible and famous. Success is everything to them. Eminent personalities like Bill Clinton, Oprah Winfrey, Paul McCartney, Tom Cruise, Barbra Streisand, Michael Jordan, Shirley MacLaine, Denzel Washington, Tiger Woods, and John Edwards are most likely all Threes.

My message to all the Threes out there is that you shouldn't let others determine your worth. Don't believe that you aren't successful until someone says otherwise. You are good the way you are. You should do things that make you feel happy. Don't do them because others think it's cool. You can never find true happiness if you let others decide what is good or bad. You can choose for yourself and have some faith in yourself. Don't live your life according to the expectations of others. Take some time and think about the things you like and the things you want. Without your success, who are you?

Type 4: The Individualist

Type Four, known as the Individualist, or the Romantic, are undoubtedly perfect for romantic relationships. Type Four consists of all those who give priority to their relationships over everything else in their lives. Regardless of whether Fours are single or in a relationship, they dedicate most of their energy towards their relationships. If you want to know if you are a Four, then you should analyze your childhood. Fours try to build their identity around how different they are from everyone else.

Have you ever wondered if you were probably switched at birth? As funny as it sounds, Romantics often like to think that they were. Fours often feel that their parents never understood their "real persona." Not just that, they often feel misunderstood by their families. Fours tend to think that there is something wrong with them and this starts their lifelong quest to find their true identity. They tend to focus on all those things that they think are missing in their relationships. Instead of feeling grateful for the things that do go right, they search for things that don't seem right to them. Fours tend to doubt their identity, and it makes them appear mysterious and intriguing to others. They hope that they will find someone who will love them for who they are. Well, that does sound quite confusing. How can anyone love you for who you are if you aren't sure of it yourself?

The primary fear that all those who possess this personality type harbor is that they don't have an identity of their own and that they aren't of any significance. They desire to express themselves and create an identity for themselves. Fours are quite compassionate, creative, sensitive, and imaginative. At their absolute worst, they seem withdrawn, melancholic, and even self-absorbed. Often, people think that Fours are moody and like to alienate themselves from others. Fours want to believe that they are unique.

One thing motivates Fours more than anything else in their quest to understand themselves: Fours constantly try to "find" themselves. Famous personalities who seem like Type Fours are Tennessee Williams, Cher, Bob Dylan, Ingmar Bergman, Soren Kierkegaard, Rudolph Nureyev, Judy Garland, Maria Callas, Edgar Allen Poe, Jeremy Irons, James Dean, Frederic Chopin, and Paul Simon.

My message to all the Fours out there is that you should let go of your imaginary self-image and should instead express yourself to others. No one will understand you if you don't try to express yourself. Accept your flaws and realize that there is nothing wrong with you. Flaws make us human, and if you have flaws, it merely means that you are human too! Learn to see who you are and accept yourself. You cannot find true love if you don't love yourself.

Type 5: The Observer

Type Fives are among the most elusive personality types and are known as the Investigators. Most Fives don't like the limelight, and they are instead happy to stay on the sidelines. They want to immerse themselves in their world of observations, and they gain confidence when they can internalize the knowledge they gain. They like to know how the world works. In short, they like to observe more than anything else. Fives have an inherent thirst for knowledge, and they want to know it all. They tend to use their relentless pursuit of knowledge to mask their insecurities.

Fives often think that they don't possess the ability to do things as well as others. Instead of trying to do something to rectify this situation, Fives tend to withdraw into their minds, their haven. They like their shell, and it gives them a sense of security and stability. Fives are often drawn to things that are somewhat unusual, less explored, and even unthinkable. Familiarity doesn't comfort them.

In your childhood, did you not feel safe in your home? No, not that you had an abusive childhood or anything of that sort. But did your parents overwhelm you? Did you feel the need to retreat into your private space? Did you, and do you, still spend a lot of time immersed in your imaginary world? A world that's full of books, music, and computers? If yes, then it is quite likely that you are a Five. Fives don't fall into what others perceive to be "normal." They define their world, and they are quite happy in it. They want to create their niche where they can be independent and confident.

The primary fear that all Fives have is that they cannot do things and that they are incompetent. Their fundamental desire is to be capable and competent in life. At their best, all Fives are quite perceptive, curious, and inventive. They are often thought of as intellectuals and intense. At their absolute worst, Fives can be detached, cynical, eccentric, and even abrasive.

Key motivations in life for Fives are the desire to control their environment with understanding, to prevent the intrusion of others, and to have the intellect and the security they desire. Albert Einstein, Vincent Van Gogh, Georgia O'Keefe, Stephen Hawking, Bill Gates, Isaac Asimov, Stanley Kubrick, Emily Dickenson, James Joyce, John Lennon, Jane Goodall, Bobby Fischer, Frederick Nietzsche, Lily Tomlin, and Stephen King all seem like Type Fives.

My message to all the Fives is that it is time you step into the real world. Don't ignore other things in your pursuit of knowledge. You don't have to retreat into your mind to escape the world. Learn to become engaged in your life and live your life. If you don't take any action, you cannot obtain any results. There is so much more to life than the world you have created for yourself. Don't run away from things, and learn to face them instead. Fives possess great intellect. Instead of being observers all the time, you should take action. Don't withdraw yourself from reality. However, it doesn't mean that the world doesn't need any Fives. Where would we all be without the discoveries and inventions of great scientists?

Type 6: The Loyalist

Type Six personalities often tend to have a down to earth approach towards life. They are a breath of fresh air when compared to all the lofty and idealistic views that other personality types tend to hold about life. They value safety and security more than anything else. Sixes are loyal friends. Not just that, they are loyal to their beliefs as well. Once they make up their mind about something and they believe in it, they will defend their belief at all costs. They are loyal to others, and they expect the same in return. They might seem brave on the exterior, but they lack self-confidence when they are no longer in their comfort zone.

Do you spend a lot of time thinking about the challenges that life throws your way? Do you fear to make big decisions by yourself? Do you usually depend on others for guidance? At the same time, do you hate it when others make decisions for you? You don't like to let others take the reins of your life, do you? If yes, then you indeed are a Six. Sixes like their security and safety. If they fail to create this, they tend to become anxious.

The underlying fear that plagues this personality type is that they will be left without any support or guidance. Sixes like their support system and it is all that they desire. At their best, all Sixes are quite confident, courageous, committed, and reliable. The traits that are usually associated with a Six are loyal (duh!), anxious, and dutiful. At their worst, this type can be very confused, indecisive, defensive, and submissive as well. You need to believe that you are a dependable and a committed person; only then will others think the same.

A couple of things that seem to motivate this personality type is their desire to be liked, their need to follow the rules, and the approval of others. Robert F. Kennedy, Tom Hanks, Malcolm X, Richard Nixon, George H.W. Bush, Bruce Springsteen Princess Diana, Richard Cheney, Woody Allen, Julia Roberts, Diane Keaton, and Gloria Steinem seem like likely candidates for this type of personality.

My advice to all the Sixes out there is that you should let go of all the anxieties you harbor. The world isn't as bad as you seem to think. Let go of all the ambivalences you nurture. You like it when others support you. However, at the same time, you are put off when others get too involved in your life. You enjoy your space, and it is okay. You should learn to draw a line between comfort and stress. Learn to express yourself. It is the only way in which you can get what you want. Learn to trust yourself. Listen to your gut and don't ignore it. It is better to depend on yourself than others.

Type 7: The Enthusiast

The Type Seven, or the Enthusiast is the busy and fun-loving type of personality. They are quite spontaneous and versatile. You can never take a Seven's sense of adventure. These optimistic souls approach life with a sense of curiosity.

Everything seems to fascinate them. These fun-loving and playful personalities are like a breath of fresh air. They are always up for an adventure. Do you have that one friend who is always up for any random plan, from going on an exotic vacation to shopping at Target! They are pretty much up for anything, and their enthusiasm levels don't seem to diminish. Are you that friend? Boredom is a word that isn't familiar to Sevens. Variety and activity help them to escape the clutches of the mundane life that most of us seem to be trapped in.

Sevens' thought processes are anticipatory—they foresee events and come up with ideas on the go; they favor activities that stimulate their mind, and this, in turn, gives them more things to think about. Well, this is a never-ending cycle. The rush of a new idea is quite thrilling for Sevens. They are happy when they can be spontaneous. Instead of spending a lot of time on one task or thought, they will instead do multiple things. Sevens experience anxiety when they aren't in touch with their inner voice that guides them.

To cope with the stress they feel, they will try to do different things to distract their minds, and it means that they have more negative feelings due to their detachment from their consciousness. Sigh! Being a Seven might be exhausting. All their energy and enthusiasm cannot do them any good if they are not in touch with their consciousness. They crave stimulation, they thrive when there is change, and they need to be on the move, always. They can keep up with a ton of activity that would otherwise exhaust the other personality types. Sevens are full of energy, and they don't like it when others feel low. They tend to go out of their way to cheer others up. They are the sorts who will happily turn the lemons into lemonade and do it with a smile.

During their childhood, most o Sevens tend to feel that they need to take care of themselves. It doesn't mean that their parents or primary caregivers were negligent. It merely says that due to certain situations, Sevens believe that they need to nurture themselves. As they start to become independent, Sevens tend to focus on transitional objects. Transitional objects is the term that psychologists use to describe things that serve as distractions to cope with anxiety. Sevens try hard to find transitional objects so that they don't have to deal with any emotional conflicts or fears.

The primary fear that all Sevens harbor is the feeling of being trapped. They fear that they will be stuck in pain and deprivation. Their primary desire is to feel content and to fulfill all their needs. A Seven at their best is enthusiastic, acquisitive, and energetic. Their love for transitional objects makes them seem somewhat materialistic and excessive. At their worst, they can be impulsive, erratic, and manic too. Stop thinking that something is wrong in the present moment. If you feel as if something is wrong, maybe you should spend some time and try to analyze the situation to find out the cause of anxiety that you experience.

The one thing that motivates a Seven more than anything else is a sense of freedom to live without any obligations or constraints. Sevens want to have fun and experience life to the fullest. All their actions boil down to these motivational factors. Famous personalities like Robin Williams, Bette Midler, John F. Kennedy, Steven Spielberg, Mozart, Lauren Bacall, Goldie Hawn, Federico Fellini, Jim Carrey, Benjamin Franklin, Elizabeth Taylor, Jack Nicholson, Lucille Ball, and Mick Jagger are perfect candidates for the type Seven personality.

My message to all the Sevens is to slow down for a while. There is no rush, and you don't have to be on the move all the time. Take some time and learn to connect with your inner self. Learn to enjoy the moment instead of thinking about all sorts of distractions. It is okay to stay still for a while and learn to make your peace with life. You can make better use of energy if you can focus. Practice meditation to gain control of your thoughts. You should control your thoughts, and it should never be the other way around.

Type 8: The Challenger

Type Eights are quite intense and expressive. Even Fours are intense and passionate, but they tend to be more sensitive and emotional about it. However, Eights can be very direct and powerful. Eights are quite a challenge. As their name suggests, they love lively discussions and thrive when they have to overcome a problem. They never shy away from a confrontation and meet it head-on. Type Eights are powerful, almost dominating, confident, decisive, willful, and slightly confrontational. They love challenges and view them as an opportunity to improve themselves. They are very charismatic and have the psychological ability to sway others to follow them. Eights are honest, open, and straightforward. They value their independence and love to make decisions on their own.

The willpower and energy that Eights possess are infectious. At an early age, Eights learn to develop their strength, will, and the endurance necessary to survive in this world. Eights don't like to be controlled by others, and they don't appreciate the thought that someone can have power over them. They are the captain of their ship, and they will not like it any other way. They are proud individualists. Eights might seem quite tough on the surface, but they are human too. They feel hurt and experience rejection like all of us. The only difference is that they will never speak about their vulnerabilities. They don't just avoid talking about their vulnerabilities; they won't even like to accept their vulnerabilities. It means that they have a little trouble receiving and giving love.

Most Eights seem to take on the role of an adult quite early in their life. They realize that it is not a good thing to be gentle in this unmerciful world. Their outlook towards life is quite bleak. They are always on their guard. They do not like to let their guard down, because if they do, they become vulnerable. Do you remember Tony Soprano from *The Sopranos*? Well, he is the perfect example of this personality type.

The primary fear that all Eights harbor is of being controlled and betrayed. They like to protect themselves and their independence. They have a strong sense of self-preservation. At their best, they are courageous, heroic, and resourceful.

However, their best traits become their shortcomings eventually. At their worst, they can be dictatorial and hard-hearted. Often, they come across as bullies.

The things that motivate them are their desire to protect the weak, to have control over their life, and their will to wield power.

Famous personalities like Martin Luther King, Jr., Mikhail Gorbachev, Franklin D. Roosevelt, Sean Connery, Lyndon Johnson, Indira Gandhi, Nelson Mandela, Anwar Sadat, Toni Morrison, Barbara Walters, Susan Sarandon, Golda Meier, Pablo Picasso, and Frank Sinatra seem to possess all the traits of a Type Eight personality.

My message to all the Eights is to open themselves up. Being soft and gentle is okay. It doesn't mean that you are weak. There is nothing wrong with being vulnerable. There is nothing more beautiful than opening up to another person. Learn to trust others a little. Letting others in is okay. Getting hurt is a part of life, of growing up. You don't have to worry about control all the time. Trust that you have a role to play in life.

Type 9: The Mediator

The final personality type in the Enneagram is that of a Mediator or Peacemaker. This personality type encompasses all the other categories. They can have the strength of Eight, the enthusiasm and energy of a Seven, the dutifulness of a Six, the intellect of a Five, the creativity of a Four, a Three's will to achieve, the generosity of a Two, and the idealism of a One. It is quite tricky for Nines to determine their personality since they feel that they can relate to all the personality types in the Enneagram. They are so empathetic that they have a tough time differentiating their feelings from those of others.

Nines often crave a stronger identity of their own. The best profession that is suited for Nines is that of a counselor. Nines are receptive, agreeable, and complacent. They are known as Peacemakers because they spend most of their time achieving internal and external peace. They love harmony more than anything else.

The basic fear of a Peacemaker is separation and loss. Nines crave peace of mind and a sense of wholeness. At their best, they are accepting, good-natured, and extremely reassuring. The adjectives that describe this type the best are complacent, compliant, and self-effacing. They might come across as slightly disengaged from time to time. The negative traits of this personality type are that they can be passive, ineffectual, and even numb. All the Nines out there, you need to understand that you are okay even when others around you aren't. The state of being of others shouldn't bother you to the extent that it disturbs your mental peace. The thing that motivates this personality type is their desire to live in peace and harmony with others. Abraham Lincoln, Walt Disney, Carl Jung, Whoopi Goldberg, Ron Howard, Gerald Ford, George Lucas, Audrey Hepburn, Walter Cronkite, Garrison Keillor, Kevin Costner, Jim Henson, Queen Elizabeth II, and Norman Rockwell are all likely to be Nines.

My message to all the Nines out there is to understand yourself. It is good that you can understand others, but how well do you know yourself? Take some time and think about the feelings you experience and the thoughts that you think. Are these your thoughts and feelings or are these the reflections of those around you? Your love for peace is terrific, but understand that you cannot bring peace to everyone around you. Learn to be content with yourself. Whenever something bothers you, take a moment to think about whether you can do something about it or not. If you cannot do anything to change the situation, then you shouldn't let it bother you.

Eleven behavior tips for the Nine Enneagram's

If you want to lead a better life, regardless of the Enneagram personality types, here are a couple of things that you can try. Here are the ten behaviors that can help change your life and will make you a happy person.

1. Not everything in your life will go precisely in the manner that you have planned. There will be setbacks. Things happen. You might mess things up. Obsessing too much over things and making your happiness dependent on outcomes will do you no good whatsoever. You need to learn to be happy, come what may. People tend to get in their way. We do this without realizing it. So you need to quit worrying about a specific outcome.

2. Things will happen, and there will be things that are beyond your control. The only thing you control is your

actions. You cannot control the situations you are in. You should stop worrying about obtaining a specific result. Instead, concentrate on the manner in which you can make the most of what's given to you. If you try too hard to get a particular result, you will tend to get in your own way. Desperation will not get you the results you want. It will hinder your growth. Stop trying to fit in where you don't belong. If the shoe doesn't fit, it is time to move on. Find something that you are comfortable with.

3. No two human beings are alike. So why should we all have just one standard for measuring success? All of us end up getting stuck in the rat race that the society has created towards achieving the so-called rules of "success" that are set by the community. There will always be someone that's better than you at something. There will never be sufficient time to do everything. Instead, you should focus on the things you opt for.

4. When you select something, you have simultaneously rejected something else. It is the norm of life, and it is entirely all right to do so. It is quite enjoyable to choose what you want to do. You need to define what happiness, success, and wealth mean to you. You cannot let society decide what you need or think you need. If that's the case, then you will always fall short of something or the other. You need to stop comparing yourself to others and stop competing with others. It is the only manner in

which you will get ahead in life. Pull yourself out of the endless rat race and the rut you are stuck in.

5. How many times have you told yourself "just this once"? Most of us have convinced ourselves that we are capable of breaking our own rules. We always find reasons to justify these small choices we make. None of these things feel like a significant decision initially. However, over a period, these things end up forming a part of the bigger picture. Human beings are good at sabotaging themselves. People tend to behave in a manner that goes against their goals or their ideals. The gap between what you do and what you should be doing should be as small as possible. The more modest this gap is, the happier you will be in life. Giving 100 percent commitment is more comfortable than giving 98 percent.

6. When you have committed yourself fully to something this means that the decision has already been made. Unless and until you are fully committed to something, you will always end up being a victim of all the external circumstances in life. If you rely on your willpower, it is more likely that you will end up crumbling. You might think that you are doing better than what you are doing. But you needn't rely on your willpower once you have given your 100 percent commitment. Regardless of the circumstances, your decision has been made. It is all about being proactive instead of being reactive.

7. Abundance, and the lack of it, tend to exist simultaneously in our life. It is always our choice which of these things we tend to. When you have decided to focus your energy on what you have in your life instead of focusing on things that are missing, happiness is a straightforward concept. It can be as simple as gratitude that you feel. According to research, there are specific physical, psychological, and social benefits of feeling gratitude. These benefits include a stronger immune system, reduction in body aches and pains, better blood pressure, and better sleep too. The psychological benefits are increased feelings of positivity; you'll feel more alert, experience more joy, and be more optimistic.

8. The social benefits are that you will feel more helpful, generous, compassionate, forgiving, outgoing, and less isolated. In spite of all these benefits, most people are usually ungrateful. People tend to focus too much of their time and attention on what they don't have. The grass always does appear to be greener on the other side. If there's one thing that you want, after achieving it, there will be something else. There is no end to this ever-growing list of wants. Life has become a constant race of having the best of things. How can you ever be happy when all you want from life is more things? Take a moment and appreciate what you have.

9. Be conscious of the language that you use. People who are grateful make use of different words like gifts, abundance, blessings, fortune, fortunate, and blessed

more frequently. If you start incorporating these words into your daily vocabulary, you will realize that the list of things that you need to be grateful for keeps on increasing. It will allow you to understand and appreciate the abundance that is present all around you. Smile a lot and say thank you when someone does something for you. It could be something as simple as acknowledging someone for holding the door open for you.

10. Giving up on the good we possess to pursue the best in life is a good strategy. There are a lot of things in life that are good, and even great. It doesn't mean that you should do them all. Every day, you are faced with once-in-a-lifetime opportunities.

11. Most people tend to grab onto any great opportunity that comes their way, even though it is not in synchronicity with their vision in life. It is the reason why the lives of people tend to move in different directions. They can't move in a single direction on a conscious level. On the contrary, happy people will refuse any opportunity, however incredible it is, as long as they are at peace with themselves. They won't sacrifice their freedom for the sake of security. They won't let distractions divert their attention. There are only specific things in life that can be described as the very "best." You are the only one that gets to decide what's best for you. Don't keep yourself occupied with the so-called "good" activities and miss out on the amazing ones.

Happy people are the ones that live in the present. They don't let go of those moments that matter. They are always grateful for what they have. Happy people focus on those aspects of their life that are significant.

Chapter Three:
Enneagram in Love

When it comes to love, does compatibility matter? A standard line that almost all those who have ever gone through a breakup use is "in the end, we weren't compatible." Compatibility might sound quite vague, but it can mean a lot of things. It can mean any of the following things:

We used to annoy each other to the extent that we weren't fond of each other towards the end. We didn't share or respect each other's values. Our expectations didn't match. Our conflicts baffled our love for each other. We didn't know how to deal with our conflicts.

Compatibility can mean anything, and it differs from one person to the other. So, what exactly does being compatible mean? According to the dictionary, it denotes the ability to live in harmony without any conflicts. It is quite impossible to maintain a relationship that is devoid of all conflicts. Conflicts are common in all relationships in life, from your family, friends, to any romantic relationship. It is kind of surprising when you think about it, isn't it, that the person that we used to think the world of suddenly becomes someone who doesn't even seem like a friend anymore?

When a relationship ends, the feeling of sympathy that you feel towards the person seems to disappear altogether. If you want a long-term relationship to last, then there needs to be a balance between novelty and comfort. It is ironic when, at times, both familiarity and novelty become quite irritating in a relationship. We all know the story. A couple falls in love. She falls for him because he is fun to be around and caring like her father was, maybe steady and sensitive as well. He falls in love with her because she is caring and nurturing like his mother, and she seems to be up for an adventure. Well, that does sound like an ordinary couple, doesn't it? Yes, it is good initially. After a couple of months or maybe years though, they feel tricked. They feel that there was false advertising on both sides.

Where has her sense of adventure gone? Why has he become uncaring? Why don't they share the same interests anymore? She likes to shop and gossip, while he likes to play golf with his buddies. Oh my, where did that ideal relationship go? Where did their shared values go? They seem to be getting on each other's nerves for every little thing.

It is painful when the person you turned to for comfort seems like your persecutor. These frustrations are an indication of the direction in which you and your partner should grow. However, what is quite tragic is that instead of working on these problems like a team, most of us make it about our suffering. Therefore, we use the term "incompatible."

The first thing that you need to understand is that conflicts are inevitable. Fights are normal, and they are bound to happen. If you want your relationship to mature, then you should expect a couple of rows now and then. The more things you have in common with your partner, the less disturbing and persistent the conflicts will seem. If you share common views about upbringings, demographics, and even world-views, the conflicts won't look too distressing. It doesn't mean that you shouldn't have any differences in opinions. Everyone has different ideas, and the difference in views is what causes conflicts. Conflicts are healthy, and you must expect them. The one thing that you should focus on is resolving the disputes that come up. A conflict doesn't mean the end of a relationship.

In fact, it is an opportunity for the couple to understand each other better. Don't think of conflict as a feeling of friendship or the lack of conflicts. Maybe it is time to change the way we look at compatibility these days. Even when we don't feel the fondness for the other, there might still be some compatibility left. If you can interpret the reason for the dissatisfaction instead of making it about personal suffering, it might help.

There are different styles of conflict, and they can be categorized into four categories. The four styles of conflict are avoidant, validating, hostile, and volatile. The only couples who are in real trouble are the ones that fall into the hostile category. Everything else can be managed with a little mutual understanding.

The one question that bothers most of us is "did I pick the right person?" Well, how can we pick someone perfect, when we are flawed? No one is perfect and to expect perfection from others is foolhardy. You might be wondering where the Enneagram fits in with all this. Well, have a little patience. There are different types of personalities, and each has its own good and bad traits. You need to understand that regardless of the type compatibility you share, relationships all boil down to how the partners deal with conflict.

There is no such thing as a perfect couple. If you still believe in that concept, you should give up on it. Instead, you should focus on different aspects of your relationship and try to make it better. According to the Enneagram, there are 45 possible combinations. For instance, One with a One, One with a Two, One with a Three, One with a Four, and so on. Some might wonder what a particular pairing works better than the rest. A type combination cannot predict the success of a relationship.

Every Enneagram type has specific imbalances in a relationship. A couple of common shortcomings are listed below. Remember that it isn't an exhaustive list. If you feel that you and your partner have any of these imbalances, then you can try to work things out slowly.

Type Ones tend to love control. They can be controlling and criticizing in a relationship to the extent that the other person can feel dejected. If you are a Type One, then don't try to micromanage things. Let go of a little control and trust your partner.

Type Twos are givers. It is in their nature to help others. However, if you are a Type Two and you ignore your needs for long, it will lead to resentment. Resentment can sour a relationship quicker than anything else. If you have specific expectations, it is best if you talk about them with your partner.

All Type Threes try to bypass their emotions. As a Type Three person, when you ignore your feelings, it will make you feel lonely and empty, even when there isn't a reason for you to feel so. If you feel something, discuss it with your partner.

Type Fours are individualists. As a Type Four person, it is good to retain your identity in a relationship, and you shouldn't give up on it. However, too much individualism can make your partner feel left out. Don't spend too much time mulling about what you feel, after all, you aren't the only one that feels things.

All Type Fives need to stop withdrawing themselves from their partners. It can make your partner feel anxious. Independence is good, but remember that you are a team. You cannot have a successful relationship if you both act as individual entities all the time.

Type Six personalities have issues with anxiety, so much so that others can feel tested and mistrusted. A Sixes doubts and unnecessary fears shouldn't be the reason for their partner's sleepless nights. If you're a Six, it is critical that you tell your partner about the things that trouble you.

Type Sevens love to multitask and spend a lot of time thinking about the future. However, Sevens, when you spend all your time thinking about a future that might or might not happen, you ignore your presence. Learn to live in the moment.

Type Eights don't like to feel vulnerable. Whenever they feel a slight vulnerability creeping in, they tend to shut others away. All you type Eight personalities, don't push your partner away. If you behave like they aren't wanted, they will soon assume that you don't need them.

Type Nines love harmony. They love peace more than anything. It means that they try to shy away from conflicts. Nines, you cannot ignore disputes all the time. If you want a healthy relationship, you need to learn to discuss things with your partner.

If you want a better relationship, then here are a couple of simple things that will help you along the way.

Hear

You need to make sure that you are both physically and mentally present when your partner is speaking to you. Let down your defenses and open your heart. You must try and understand your partner so that you can fulfill their needs. It's not verbal communication that you need to watch out for, but non-verbal communication as well. Notice whether your partner is angry, the expression in their eyes, body language, hand gestures, and tone of voice. It will help you understand what your partner is feeling. Your partner needs to reciprocate the same as well.

Empathize

Once you are confident that you understand what your partner is feeling, you need to pay attention towards the feelings that you have when you observe your partner. It is essential to search for the tender and the softer feelings towards your partner. Can you connect with your partner on a deeper level and feel pain when your partner is in pain? Can you be compassionate towards your partner and let your partner know the same? Your first instinct might be to offer advice or try and solve the problem when you know that your partner is in distress. Though your intentions are good, this comes across as being judgmental or even critical. Instead, the pure expression of compassion can soothe your partner's distress and calm them down as well. More than advice, this is what your partner might need most of the times.

Act

You will need not only to take action to deal with your partner's needs and concerns but will also have to show that you are willing to change. These actions needn't be anything elaborate; they can be something as simple as helping with chores around the house, calling your partner during the day because you miss them, and perhaps spending less money when you know your partner gets anxious about it. When your partner can see that you are taking the concerns they express seriously, your partner will feel valued and respected. It will initiate a positive cycle where your partner will appreciate you and you will understand your partner. You needn't be perfect; you do need to act in a manner that shows that you care and that you are trying to change.

Love

You need to feel and express your unconditional love towards your partner. You need to deliberately make some space in your life if you want to reconnect with your partner. Even if the recent interactions that you had with your partner left you feeling angry and distant, you need to make an effort if you want your marriage to survive. Think of all the good qualities that your partner has, the ones that made you love them initially. Go through your photo albums or think of those times when you felt that you had everything that you ever wished for and more. You need to find a way to not just forgive the mistakes you made but also the ones that your partner made, the errors that pushed you off track.

The feeling of love that you have towards your partner—what does it make you do? You might want to reach out and express your love towards your partner in a physical form or might want to do something special like taking them for a meal to their favorite restaurant or anything that you can think of. Your expression of love shouldn't depend on how your partner reacts, but it should be unconditional. If you think there's a particular issue that's holding you back from expressing your unconditional love, care, support, and trust towards your partner, then you need to take steps to get these issues sorted out.

Respect

Respect is critical when it comes to building a healthy relationship. You must make the effort of understanding and respecting all your partner's interests. Even if some things are not to your liking, you cannot ask them to quit it; this will not lead to a sustainable and lasting relationship. Your partner must reciprocate the respect, for the relationship to work out.

Empathy

Remember that there is no room for selfishness in a relationship and empathy takes center stage. Empathy refers to understanding your partner's point of view and providing comfort. If you showcase humanity and compassion, then your partner is sure to feel attracted to you and will reciprocate.

Trust

One of the most critical foundational stones of a healthy relationship is trust. Both you and your partner must trust each other and give one another enough room to make independent decisions. Interfering in each other's matters or lack of trust can all lead to cracks in the relationship. It can start off as a small complaint and become more prominent with time.

Loyalty

This one goes without saying. If you want your relationship to last and work out, then you must be loyal to your partner. It is in human nature to be tempted, but what is essential is having love and respect for your partner and doing right by them.

Chapter Four:
Physical Appearance

Did you know that your physical appearance could give others signs of your personality type? All those who belong to a specific Enneagram type tend to share certain physical similarities as well. In this section, you will learn about the general physical appearance of each of the Enneagram types.

Type One

The physical appearance of most of the Ones is such that it represents their inner dryness. Ones often tend to be thin and lean, at times to the extremes. Male Ones tend to prefer a beard or mustache. In some extreme cases, Ones can be obese too, but it is quite rare. They are usually tall, stand up straight, and use limited gestures. Ones tend to have an aura of being spare and rigid. Their smiles are often restrained but whenever they smile, it is always genuine. Ones like neatness and order, and the same shows in their physical appearance as well.

Type Two

Twos tend to opt for clothes that are conservative yet stylish. Neatness is very important for them. Twos are often elegant, poised, and like to add a little color to their outfit in a manner that is quietly distinctive – something like a colorful tie or an item of statement jewelry. In a social setting, Twos seem a little formal. Men and women with this Enneagram type like to be well groomed always.

Type Three

Threes like to look their fashionable best. Their clothes are always well chosen and reflect the current fashion trends. Threes are conscious of their weight, and they would never let themselves become obese. The clothes they opt for often express their calm and cheerful nature. Threes also like to look attractive and sexy.

Type Four

Fours like to present themselves to the world artfully and tastefully. Their idea of fashion often involves the combination of black with other cheerful colors. They usually have a medium build. Did you ever come across men and women dressed in outrageous costumes? Well, if you did, then it is highly likely that they were a Four or a Seven (more on that later).

Type Five

Fives are usually not too keen on their appearance. The best way to describe a five will be reasonable, ordinary, and nothing too bold. Most of the Fives tend to have glasses. Fives tend to carry a disheveled look. Fives with a strong Four wing tend to love interesting items of clothing. There is a strong chance that a person with messy hair and askew spectacles is a Type Five.

Type Six

Sixes have an innate desire to be likable and appealing. There are only two extremes that Sixes have - they can either be extremely attractive or scruffy and nothing in between. Sixes like to project that they are tough, even when they aren't. It is entirely unintentional that their body language comes across as being defensive or accusatory.

Type Seven

Sevens can be quite vain but their clothing options are usually gender-neutral. Sevens love color and they want to be noticed. They tend to lack the finesse that a Four has when it comes to fashion. So, the clothes that a Seven opts for are often loud and over the top. Aesthetics aren't something that Sevens can be bothered with.

Type Eight

Eights take a lot of care about their appearance. Slick and well dressed are the two common adjectives that perfectly describe an Eight. However, the way they dress depends on their mood and situations. For instance, when an Eight is happy and feels empowered, he looks quite elegant and dapper. However, if he isn't in a good mood, then it's the exact opposite. Eights mood dictates the way they present themselves. Most of them tend to have large features and a rough or rugged look.

Type Nine

Nines tend to be physically big. They are blessed with long and solid bones. Their movements are fluid and graceful when they are at ease. If a Nine is disturbed, he often comes across as being clumsy and uncoordinated. Their fashion choices are often tradition and are seldom loud or flashy. Nines don't crave for attention, and their sense of style represents the same.

Well, it isn't quite easy to identify someone's Enneagram type solely based on his or her looks. However, the points discussed in this chapter will come in handy to identify the person and their enneagram. Once you learn to identify Enneagram personalities, you will soon be able to find certain physical similarities among the same types.

Conclusion

I would like to thank you once again for purchasing this book. I hope it proved to be an informative and an enjoyable read.

By now you may have figured out your personality type and the traits you possess. Now you can work to easily improve your plus points and reduce your negative characteristics. Remember that the Enneagram is a way to understand yourself better. However, you cannot expect any change if you don't make use of the information provided in this book.

Take some time to contemplate your life. There are different personality types, and each has its good and bad points. No one is flawless. You need to understand yourself better if you want to improve your life. Self-awareness is necessary for growth and development. Now that you know yourself better, you can understand others as well. Thank you, and all the best.

Did you enjoy this book so far?

Anyone can improve the quality of their life by becoming aware of their and other's driving forces. So they'll not only know the differences in the way people see each other but can also accept it and use it for the benefit of their own and for others.

We are in a world full of diversity, surrounded by people with unique personalities, talents, motivations, and minds. I know that Enneagram helps to see and understand yourself and this world we live in. Both my experiences and experiences of others I've worked with prove that knowing the nine types helps you in all kinds of life situations. From self-discovery, to accepting and dealing with others Enneagram helps you to get the most out of it.

There are people reading this book that will be able to improve their lives and make a difference because of my work and effort. I'm chasing neither the fame nor the money. As a self-publisher, my mission, my personal legend is to use the knowledge and talents I have to take my part of making the world a better place.

I'm asking your help to achieve this goal. If you enjoy this book and agree with my vision, please take a moment to visit Amazon.com and leave an honest review. I'd greatly appreciate it and it would help my work to get these ideas to more who seek it.

Thank you very much!

ENNEAGRAM

----- ❧❧❦❧ -----

Embrace Your Potential and Overcome Your Weak Points

with
Enneagram Exercises, Meditations and Questions

by Eleanor Cooper

Introduction

I would like to take this opportunity to thank you for purchasing this book, "Enneagram: Embrace Your Potential and Overcome Your Weak Points with Enneagram Exercises, Meditations and Questions."

Have you ever been surprised by how some things predicted through numerology or horoscope turn out so accurate? Well, you will be amazed to know how precisely the Enneagram can describe your personality. Long ago, it was considered to be a powerful tool for personality growth. An Enneagram can throw light on your strengths and weaknesses, thereby allowing you to concentrate on improving your ideal personality. This can lead to a content and satisfied personal and professional life.

You can take an Enneagram Personality test to determine your personality from the nine distinct types. Knowing your Enneagram type can be a remarkable experience, as each personality type has a distinctive way of behaving and thinking based on the inner patterns and motivational factors. When you understand your personality type, you will be able to accomplish your real potential by letting go of all your negative traits. Clarity about your respective personality type can help you tune into the three wisdom centers – heart, belly and head.

Centuries ago, many ancient cultures had already recognized the importance of these three centers. In recent times, the neuroscientists have discovered the neurological networks in all these three areas, but what has the Enneagram got to do with the wisdom centers? Each of the nine personality types in the Enneagram is a combination of these three wisdom centers. You can try this test to know your type: check out the special gift you can find later in this book.

This book will serve as a detailed guide on Enneagram, the ways it can be used to understand your potential, overcome your flaws and acknowledge your underlying characteristics. The chapters in the book will concentrate on what Enneagram is, how it works and how it can be used.

I hope this book serves as an informative and interesting read to you!

Happy Reading!

Chapter One:
Enneagram

If you are someone who is interested in taking your personal growth and awareness level to the next stage, then *the Enneagram of Personality* (also referred to as Enneagram) is essential for you. So, what is this Enneagram all about?

It is the psychological classification model that concentrates on your personality traits. It is similar to the popular Myers Briggs model. The Myers Briggs model helps in understanding your cognitive functions, whereas the Enneagram helps in creating awareness on your main personality traits (both at a conscious and subconscious level). It will help you know more about your individual traits and the unconscious strategy that you usually apply while taking decisions. It provides you a way to observe your ego mechanisms and personality patterns more closely. This cannot be easily done and requires practice in a mindful state.

What is an Enneagram?

An Enneagram is a powerful means for you to make a collective and personal transformation. The term *Enneagram* is derived from the two Greek words *Ennea* and *Grammos* – *Ennea* means *nine* and *Grammos* means *a written symbol*. The diagrammatic representation of Enneagram is a nine-pointed symbol that represents the nine distinctive strategies that relate self, the world and the others.

Each of the nine Enneagram types has a specific pattern of feeling, thinking and acting that basically stems from the outside view or inner drive. The Enneagram promotes a better and clear understanding through a universal language that rises above culture, religion, gender and nationality. Although we are all unique in our own ways, we mostly share common experiences rooted from different causes or scenarios.

Eventually, the Enneagram is an *inside job* that determines your type and helps you recognize your focus on your own understanding, core beliefs, development path and coping strategies. The fundamental value of the Enneagram comes from identifying the depth of your behavioral patterns and the way it relates to your focus of impulse, personal experience and awareness. It is not just based on your external behaviors, but has more to do with your internal mold.

The diagrammatic representation of the Enneagram structure might look complicated, but it is actually quite simple. Here is how it goes:

Draw a circle. Mark nine points at equal distances on its circumference. Assign each point by a number – 1 to 9. Let nine be at the top for uniformity and by rule. Each of these nine points represents the nine basic personality types. You will also need to connect all the nine points with each other through the inner lines of the Enneagram. You should connect the points in the following way:

- Points 3, 6 and 9 will have to form an equilateral triangle.

- Point 1 connects with 4, 4 with 2, 2 with 8, 8 with 5, 5 with 7 and 7 with 1.

- The six points (1, 4, 2, 8, 5, and 7) will form an irregular hexagram.

Chapter Two:
Explore the Nine Types

The nine Enneagram types describe the personality and behavioral patterns of an individual. Concentrating on the three important elements (the psychological aspect, spiritual aspect and somatic aspect) helps to understand your personality better and paves way for a positive development structure. We will see more about these three elements in the next chapter.

There are three other centers of perception and intelligence when it comes to knowing your strengths and weaknesses:

- Head (The Intellectual Center)

- Heart (The Emotional Center)

- Body (The Instinctual Center)

Although every one of us experiences all three, each Enneagram personality type has a *home base* in one of them, or maybe a specific strength that associates with one of them. This prime center persuades the way you live in this world. It is the key factor that helps you to develop your potential and overcome the blind spots. When you balance all the three centers, it helps in achieving a well-balanced and peaceful life.

Head (The Intellectual Center)

The Enneagram types – 7, 6 and 5 form the head center, which is also referred to as the *Intellectual Center*. People belonging to this type are the *thinking-types* who mostly gather information, figure out things, have ideas and are rational, while taking decisions before they get ready to act. They primarily focus on creating safety and certainty, or work to find multiple alternatives (just in case one doesn't work).

Type 7 – The Epicure

7s believe that it is necessary to keep your possibilities open and be optimistic to lead a good life; therefore, they are adventurous and look for pleasurable options. They often like to stay unattached to avoid pain and concentrate on their own self.

Attention focus

-   Glamorous future plans.

-   Multiple options (to be on a safer side).

Lessons for life

-   To regain and accept life's pleasures and pains as in the present moment.

Style of Speaking

- Spontaneous, high-spirited, idea-oriented, logical and fast-paced.

- Perceived by others as people who keep making excuses, who are apathetic to other's views, quick in shifting topics and always self-absorbed.

Type 6 – The Loyal Skeptic

6s believe that it is necessary to have constant vigilance to live in the hazardous world that can never be trusted. According to them, safety and certainty are important to lead a peaceful life; therefore, they are excellent in problem-solving. They can be trustworthy, intuitive, curious and good friends, but they are equally snappish, apprehensive and suspicious.

Attention focus

- They think about the worst-case scenarios.

- Work on options to deal with those scenarios.

Lessons for life

- To reclaim trust in self and others.

- Live comfortably, even when there is uncertainty.

Style of Speaking

- Information-oriented, attentive, quizzical and engaging.

- Perceived by others as people who are negative, opposing, demanding, skeptical or challenging.

Type 5 – The Observer

5s believe that it is necessary to safeguard self from a world that is too demanding but gives very little; therefore, they are happy with whatever they have. They are logical, modest and thoughtful. They can also be private and completely detached and refuse to give in easily.

Attention focus

- Intellectual understanding and gathering knowledge.

- Work to do away with the potential interference from other's feelings, agendas and desires.

Lessons for life

- To reconnect to the energy of your life force and understand your deepest feelings.

- To realize the availability of the surplus resources and abundant energy in the world.

Style of Speaking

- Not interested in *small talks*.

- Clear, verbose, methodical and focused on the content.

- Perceived by others as people who are distant, detached, emotionally disconnected and over-analytical.

Heart (The Emotional Center)

The Enneagram types – 2, 3 and 4 form the heart center, which is also referred to as the *Emotional Center*. They are high on feelings and mostly have concern and compassion for others, and they believe in loyalty and romance and therefore give special attention to the heart for negative and positive feelings.

Type 2 – The Giver

2s believe that it is important to give wholly to others to be loved; therefore, they are relationship-oriented, accommodating, kind and supportive, but they can also be equally demanding, haughty and interfering.

Attention focus

- Needs, desires and feelings of others.

Lessons for life

- To develop the humbleness by allowing yourself to be loved without being too needy.

- Having your own needs and working to fulfill them.

- Open, friendly, communicative, responsive to others' needs, supportive and approachable.

- Perceived by others as people who are irksome, indignant, controlling or overly helpful.

Type 3 – The Performer

3s believe that it is important to be successful and accomplish something in your life to be loved; therefore, they are mostly goal-oriented, fast-paced, competent and hard-working. They can also be intolerant, unmindful to feelings and are always driven by success.

Attention focus

- Goals, tasks and appreciation for accomplishments.

Lessons for life

- To understand the truth that love doesn't have anything to do with success or material wealth.

- You attract love, not because of *what you do,* but because of *who you are.*

Style of Speaking

- Confident, undeviating, fast-paced, excited and topic-focused.

- Perceived by others as people who are impatient, preventive, dominant to others' views and overly efficient.

Type 4 – The Romantic

4s believe that it is possible to regain an ideal state or get back the lost love by finding a situation or love that is special, gratifying and unique; therefore, they are genuine, idealistic, and compassionate and are deeply emotional. They can also be grumpy, self-absorbed and dramatic.

Attention focus

- The missing factor (their quest for what is missing in their life).

Lessons for life

- To regain fullness by appreciating what is there in the present moment instead of overthinking on what happened in the past, or will be happening in the future.

- Accepting self as who you are without the need to be unique or special.

- Feeling the experience in your mind and body.

Style of Speaking

- Focused on self, too personal, expressive of feelings, and appreciate originality.

- Perceived by others as people who are too expressive, have deep emotions and are not completely satisfied with responses.

Body (The Instinctual Center)

The Enneagram types – 8, 9 and 1 form the body center, which is also referred to as the *Instinctual Center*. They are the *body-based types* who mostly focus on social belonging, power, personal security and taking the right action.

Type 8 – The Protector

8s believe that it is necessary to be influential and tough to assure safety and protection in the tough world; therefore, they are strong, action-oriented and straightforward. They like to be fair and seek justice whenever something goes wrong. They can also be reckless, extreme and too impactful.

Attention focus

- Getting things moving in the right direction at work or otherwise.

- Ensure others don't control them.

- Injustice.

Lessons for life

- To harness the life force in creative ways.

- Being assertive and vulnerable at the same time. Integrating both the attribute positively.

Style of Speaking

- Firm, commanding, honest, energetic and oriented to justice and truth.

- Perceived by others as people who are loud, dominating, intimidating and challenging.

Type 9 – The Mediator

9s believe that it is necessary to blend in and go with the flow to be valued and loved; therefore, they are steady, comprehensive, comfortable, friendly and easygoing. They look for harmony, but they can also get stubborn, be absentminded and evade things to avoid conflicts.

Attention focus

- External environment.

- Agendas of others (people around you).

Lessons for life

- To reclaim self.

- Wake up to your own priorities and concentrate on them.

Style of Speaking

- Friendly, focused on others' feelings and facts. They don't deal with situations aggressively.

- Perceived by others as people who are unclear, wavering, scattered and overly appeasing.

Type 1 – The Perfectionist

1s believe that it is necessary to be right and perfect to be worthy; therefore, they are responsible, self-controlled and hard working. They prefer to improve themselves based on the feedback or suggestion they receive. They can also be bitter, self-judging and critical.

Attention focus

- What is correct or incorrect – the right and the wrong.

Lessons for life

- To change things that can be changed and to accept things that cannot be changed.

- To develop the wisdom to know the difference between the acceptable and unacceptable.

Style of Speaking

- Direct, honest, specific, clear and always concentrates on the required details.

- Perceived by others as people who are closed-minded, judgmental and fixated on their opinions.

Chapter Three:
Personality Development

The Enneagram is the focal point for the three key aspects of personality development:

- Psychological (Mental or Emotional aspects)

- Spiritual (Receptiveness)

- Somatic (Instinctual neuro-pathways)

When you work on these three elements individually, you add a lot of value to your traits and underlying behavioral patterns. The Enneagram serves as a map for you to work on all these areas that create an interaction with your own self. This greatly helps in increasing the effectiveness, while working on your personality.

Type 1

Psychology

- Strong inner critic.

- Holds back his/her desires and needs.

- Outburst of anger or guilt over behaviors or impulses that they review as wrong.

- Idealistic.

- Put forth a great effort to improve the world around them.

- May come forward to work for a political or a social cause (might take on the social reformer's role).

Spirituality

- To embrace the intrinsic perfection in one's own self and in the world.

- Attain tranquility by accepting the mistakes as a natural way to grow and learn.

- Important to relax by shifting the focus from the necessity to correct every mistake (of others) to *accepting* the errors, desires, differences and the darkness.

Somatics

- A lot of physical energy.

- Ability to exercise self-control over their impulses and feelings.

- This causes physical tension in the neck, jaw, shoulders, pelvic floor and diaphragm.

Type 1 has an instinctive ability to know their belly centers, but not consciously. This is because they usually hold the tension in the diaphragm causing a hindrance in breathing.

Type 2

Psychology

- Empathize with the feelings and needs of others.

- Alert on relationships and are good to others by being supportive.

- Face difficulty in turning attention towards self and own needs.

- Emotionally sensitive.

- Want to be liked and accepted by everyone and will be willing to change themselves to get this approval.

- Challenge in setting boundaries for self.

Spirituality

- To reclaim freedom from a world that will only love and approve people if their own needs are fulfilled.

- Should learn to pay attention to one's own needs.

- Should be ready to receive from others and give only what is right.

They can experience pure joy and happiness only if they are able to give and accept love freely.

Somatics

- Energetic and expressive in the upper body.

- Difficult to sense the lower body or stay grounded.

- Talk out to release the controlled emotions and anxiety (vocally expressive).

- Show empathy to others and are receptive to their feelings.

- May restrict breathing while waiting for other's responses (while waiting for an answer or decision).

Type 3

Psychology

- Ability to take the initiative and work hard to achieve their goals to succeed.

- Highly adaptive in nature and can meet the expectations of others.

- Extremely active. Have difficulty in slowing down.

- More inclined towards material benefits and praises.

- Doesn't concentrate much on inside emotions and feelings that can be a danger to themselves.

Spirituality

- Important to remember that they are human beings and not robots without emotions and feelings.

- Need to take steps to allow their feelings to surface.

- Open up to receive love and accept who they are.

Somatics

- Holds the tension or energy in the heart area.

- Instead of giving time to their feelings, they channel it to achieve productivity by getting into action for gaining results.

- Although the emotional pressure bottles up, the lid is still on.

- Have a strong life force, but will be unable to access it unless they are given an *external push.*

- Not slowing down to feel the natural pace in their body (especially tensions in the chest area).

Type 4

Psychology

- Experience a sense of yearning or feel distressed or envy for what is missing.

- Look for depth and intensity in relationships or work.

- Always on a mission to seek their inner personal creativity.

- Most 4s are artists who are pro in expressing the universal emotions.

- Should balance grief with joy and satisfaction in order to heal self.

Spirituality

- Need to realize the importance of appreciation and acceptance.

- Should live in the present moment.

- Must understand the significance of accepting things from the inside out and not the outside in.

Somatics

- Have an emotional life, which can lead to immense pain or extreme happiness.

- Oscillate between *striving hard to get recognized* and *getting lost in their own internal world*.

- Can easily get upset and withdraw self.

- On the contrary, they tend to open up when excited or anxious or have too many feelings.

Type 5

Psychology

- Highly intellectual and knowledgeable.

- Looks for privacy as the presence of other people might be too intruding.

- Detached from emotional pressure.

- Stays away from others and gives them freedom, but, at times, they feel lonely too.

- Need to balance their withdrawal trait by reaching out to others, even if it involves conflict or embarrassment.

Spirituality

- 5s usually disengage themselves from emotional needs and feelings by withdrawing into the mind and reducing their needs.

- Reversing the process of *getting disengaged from the emotional self* is crucial.

- They can naturally hail the life energy by opening up their emotions and expanding the connection for their greater good.

Somatics

- Look to develop their expertise and improve their knowledge by protecting their independence and privacy.

- Always stay within their heads by setting aside the emotional needs or bodily sensations.

- Holds the tension in the gut region.

- Sensitive to touch, intrusion and sound.

Type 6

Psychology

- 6s use their intellect and perception to figure out people's character.

- Ability to perceive the world in a logical sense.

- Concentrates on safeguarding their community, group or project.

- Good at foreseeing problems and finding solutions.

- Keep oscillating between faith and doubt. Can be a true believer or a rebel.

- Tend to worry, put things off, get cautious and waver when anxious.

- When ready to face the cause of anxiety, they support themselves and get ready to act in order to conquer their fears.

- They can be more courageous and flexible when they learn to trust their instinct, even when there is an air of doubt or uncertainty.

Spirituality

- Got to get rid of doubt and fear by emphasizing the fact that the world is not such a threatening place to live.

- Journey to faith can be difficult, but it is a necessity.

Somatics

- Perceptive in foreseeing problems, identifying solutions and ascertaining rules for safety.

- Few are cautious, while others are in a hurry to act.

- Always on high alert mode when they sense danger signals (can be magnified, real or imaginary).

- They withdraw physically or mentally from situations that put them into an anxious mode.

- Build up rigidity and muscular tension leading to breathing issues.

- Throat and diaphragm are the control centers and 6s can have a problem in speaking (they tend to stutter) when anxious.

Type 7

Psychology

- Positive and optimistic with no limitations.

- Love to have fun while traveling and seek more adventure.

- Tend to get irritated or start criticizing when reality doesn't match with their ideologies.

- Challenging to concentrate on work or a relationship, as they cannot focus on the depth and intensity of the bond.

- Will need to balance themselves by slowing down and listening to other's suffering and their own (as well). Should be tolerant.

- Should welcome all walks of life and live in the present.

- Need to acknowledge both extremities of emotions equally – _grief, frustration, pain, boredom, fear_ and _happiness, pleasure, options, and excitement._

- Should be more empathetic with others and show gratitude.

Somatics

- Over-energetic and highly attentive.

- Experience looseness in shoulders and upper chest as the body concentrates more on avoidance (as patterns).

- The biggest challenge is to stay grounded as they often retreat from grief or pain by withdrawing into their minds.

Type 8

Psychology

- Have leadership quality as they take charge of situations.

- Fair on judging.

- Should control their excessive appetites.

Spirituality

- Should embrace virtue in people and approach every situation with an open mind.

- Should appreciate the inner truth in everyone.

- Need to learn to restrain the unlimited instinctual energy and delay the tendency to always jump into action.

Somatics

- Excellent instinctual energy.

- Always gets into the tough mode to avoid vulnerability.

- Shows chronic patterns of physical tension.

Type 9

Psychology

- Seeks harmony.

- Excellent in seeing all the perspective of life, but have a problem with inertia.

- Faces difficulty in setting priorities.

- Keep changing directions or shifting attention (they are constantly on the move).

Spirituality

- Should work towards awakening their inner self and get lively, especially during times of distress.

- Should set their own priorities and work towards the same within timelines.

- Avoid falling for secondary search (wavering) and resist from getting influenced by others.

Somatics

- Not in sync with their bodies.

- Not paying attention to the intuition that is operating in the gut.

- Holding tension in the body.

- Prefer staying undercharged and lack muscle tone.

- Low-energy individuals suffer from sluggishness and inertia, while high-energy individuals are super-active.

Chapter Four:
How does it work

You can look at the Enneagram as a set of nine distinct personality types. Each number on the Enneagram denotes one type, but it is quite common to find little of your self in almost all the nine types. But the point is, one of these nine types will stand out to be the closest to who you really are, and this becomes your *basic personality.*

You have one of these nine types dominating your personality, your inborn character and other pre-natal elements as the main determining factors of your type from childhood. Consequently, this inherent attitude fundamentally conditions the way you learn to adapt to the early childhood atmosphere; therefore, the overall course of one's personality mirrors the totality of all the childhood factors that helped in influencing its development. This includes the genetic factor as well.

How does the Enneagram work?

You need to have a basic understanding of how the Enneagram works before you try to determine your personality type. The Enneagram is basically a system with its structure represented in the form of a circle. There are arrows inside the circle that point in all the directions. The Enneagram depicts the nine personality types (ego structures) and all types are interconnected in different ways.

As mentioned earlier, each individual has a dominant type that is established in his/her childhood. It can also be before or after birth, but the definition is not clear yet. David Daniels, a famous Enneagram expert, tells that it is a combination – the type gets established both pre and post birth.

Along with the primary type, there is also a dominant wing attached to each individual and this can be one of the two types, i.e., the types on adjacent sides of the dominant wing. For instance, type 8 can be type 8 with a 9 wing or type 8 with a 7 wing. It is the wing that flavors the type. It is possible to examine your ego mechanisms in a solid way using the Enneagram.

The connection between the types doesn't end here – each will have a *stress point* (the individual will resemble this type when he or she is under stress). They also have an *integration type* (the individual will resemble all the healthy characteristics when they learn to manage the unhealthy aspect of their own type). You cannot be a pure personality type – there will be a unique mixture of your basic type and your wing type. Your basic type will dominate your overall personality, while the wing type will complement it by adding significant elements to your whole personality (which can be conflicting in some cases). You can consider your wing to be *the second side of your personality*. You will be in a better position to understand your own self only if you take both the basic type and wing type into consideration.

Wing Points and Dynamic Points

Two kinds of movement (each with a different quality) happen on the Enneagram. The movement that happens around the circumference of the circle to the points on the adjacent side of your personality type is referred to as *Wing Points*. The movement that happens inside the Enneagram to the two points that connect to your own point by a straight line is referred to as *Dynamic Points*.

Wing Points

The two points next to your own point (the home base) on the circumference of the circle are your neighbors whom you can visit easily. It naturally doesn't take much time to accept the personal style of your wing points. Although they are different from your *home base,* they are not very different, thereby allowing you to see the world through their eyes, or adapt to their habits (good and bad). When you are discovering your personality type for the first time, you might identify with both or one of your wings. It might also confuse you to the extent that you may not be able to distinguish between your basic type and wing type. This is because every type can be outlined as a combination of two wing points.

For instance, if you blend a 2 and a 4, you will come up with a 3 and, similarly, if you blend a 5 and a 7, you might end up with a 6. The point is, you can have access to both your wings and they can be helpful to you at various times with their different set of characteristics and resources. Nevertheless, some evidence confirms that one of the two wings is predominant or more recognizable. You will need to observe self to find out if you have a predominant wing or you keep moving to both the wings equally.

Regardless of the patterns, it is evident that your basic personality type is greatly influenced by your wings. This leads to various major behavioral fluctuations and changes in your perspective. This can also give you interesting variations amidst the nine types.

Dynamic Points

The movement that happens inside the Enneagram is not easy when compared to the movements that happen in your wing points. The movement that happens within the Enneagram causes a major shift in your experience – it can be temporary, but the change has a high impact on your behavioral pattern.

You will be able to notice the change in yourself, and most often people around you will notice it too. At times, these shifts can be distressing for you as you might think that you are no longer able to take control of your emotions or your behavioral patterns, but, when you start noticing these shifts and make necessary attempts to manage them well, they then can add value to your professional and personal development. When you get access to an entirely new set of resources that can add value to your character or balance your existing personality, then you are benefitted by the change.

Moving to the dynamic points can help you in the following ways:

- You are ready to step out of the box.

- You willingly expand your options.

- You don't get stuck to your habitual style.

- You develop a whole new style to respond to the world around you.

Regardless of you being in the inner triangle (with connecting points 9, 6 and 3) or on the other set of lines (with connecting points 1, 4, 2, 8, 5 and 7), you will find two lines connecting your type to two other points. For instance, if you are type 8, then you will have connecting lines to type 2 and type 5.

In the *forward* direction, you have your *resource point or the stress point* and in the other direction (*moving back*), you have your *heart point* or *the relaxation point.*

The resource point is where you get to access some of the important qualities that help you to take action – you either go to that point when you are under stress, or you go there to access the competencies and intelligence of that point. Either way, you get stressed or uncomfortable when you go to the *resource point, which* is why it is also known as *the stress point.*

The relaxation point is where you get to occupy a type that is extremely helpful for your transformation and personal growth. This is the point that holds the key to most of your underlying personality issues, often termed as the *undeveloped side* or *the shadow side.* You will have to let down your usual defenses and relax in order to open up. You should let go of your normal way of looking at the world and try to be more vulnerable and flexible to allow *the new dimension* inside you. You are able to dwell deeper within you and learn more about *your real self* when you feel secure and safe. This makes you to be more available to your loved and intimate ones.

It is indeed challenging to get in touch with the inner feelings and core issues in your relaxation point. There is a possibility to get snapped back to your personality type when you continue with the usual operating procedures and go with the familiar point of view. However, if you are able to stay long enough in your relaxation point and incorporate the essence, then you will be able to re-inhabit your personality type with more balance.

You move *forward* to your *resource point (stress point)* in one of the following ways:

- 3 goes to 9, 9 goes to 6 and 6 goes to 3, i.e., 3963.

- 1 goes to 4, 4 goes to 2, 2 goes to 8, 8 goes to 5, 5 goes to 7 and 7 goes to 1, i.e., 1428571.

Similarly, you move *backwards* to your *relaxation point (heart point)*, i.e., in the opposite direction:

- 3 goes to 6, 6 goes to 9 and 9 goes to 3, i.e., 3693.

- 1 goes to 7, 7 goes to 5, 5 goes to 8, 8 goes to 2, 2 goes to 4 and 4 goes to 1, i.e., 1758241.

Chapter Five:
How to get started

Each Enneagram type has a *forgotten or repressed* intelligence and a *supporting or primary* intelligence. The major step towards your self-development will be to reintegrate the *repressed center*. You have suppressed your *forgotten intelligence* from your conscious self since your early age. This is similar to the *Dynamic Point* theory of your *undeveloped (shadow) side in the relaxation point*. (Refer to Chapter 4.)

Your *repressed center* obstructs everything by controlling the whole show from the unconscious (or subconscious) level. For instance, if you have a repressed *thinking center (intellectual center)*, you get habituated to a particular routine and become arrogant. Similarly, if you have a repressed *feeling center (emotional center)*, you get dominated by misguided and silly emotions. Lastly, if you have a repressed *doing center (instinctual center)*, your actions are mostly misdirected.

The following table gives you a clear picture on the *repressed center* for your particular Enneagram type:

Enneagram Type	Repressed Center
Type 1 – The Perfectionist	Thinking (Intellectual) center – Head

Type 2 – The Giver	Thinking (Intellectual) center – Head
Type 3 – The Performer	Feeling (Emotional) center – Heart
Type 4 – The Romantic	Doing (Instinctual) center – Body
Type 5 – The Observer	Doing (Instinctual) center – Body
Type 6 – The Loyal Skeptic	Thinking (Intellectual) center – Head
Type 7 – The Epicure	Feeling (Emotional) center – Heart
Type 8 – The Protector	Feeling (Emotional) center – Heart
Type 9 – The Mediator	Doing (Instinctual) center – Body

You need to understand that your repressed center need not necessarily be clear from the way you interact with people. It is more to do with your inner world. For example, if *thinking* is your repressed center, you will most likely experience stagnancy while you think. It is more of your internal quality.

When you know your type's repressed center, you will need to take steps to bring them back to your conscious self. For instance, you will need to bring back your *repressed thinking center* by reading intellectual books and pushing yourself to take up ideas that ultimately challenge you. This way you will be able to *embrace your lost investigative side* and lose the *stagnancy in* the *thinking side.*

Similarly, you work on your *repressed doing center* by taking the risk to bring back your adventurous side. Likewise, you can work on your repressed feeling center by allowing yourself to experience all the emotions (especially negative ones) and acknowledging the discomfort. This way you allow yourself to feel the vulnerable side in you and work on understanding its effects on you.

Working on the Points

Point 1 – The Perfectionist

Wing Points

1s have two wings – 9 and 2.

<u>Predominant 9 wing</u>

- Oriented towards balance and harmony.

- 1s drive to get things right gets mediated by the desire to be comfortable.

- Tend to calm down by adopting a slow pace.

- Drawback: 9 wing can set the 1s to be flexible or less adaptable to others' needs.

- Advantage: Steady productivity with attention on quality.

Predominant 2 wing

- Drawn towards relationships.

- Being helpful and supportive.

- 1s are expressive when 2 wing is active.

- Drawback: Gets upset or anxious due to interpersonal conflicts or when others are not doing things right.

- Advantage: Perfect combination of organizational and people skills.

Dynamic Points

1s have two dynamic points – 7 (relaxation point) and 4 (resource point).

Relaxation point – 7

- Open to multiple possibilities.

- More tolerant towards multiple plans.

- Less judgmental and critical about self and others.

- 1s find it easier to go with the flow and have fun when they relax into the 7. Loosens the physical tension.

- In case the relaxation point is not integrated well, 1s tend to lose control and might indulge in excessive drinking habits.

- In case 1s succeed to integrate with 7, 1s hold the positivity and enthusiasm of the 7, along with the hard work and responsibility of their own point (1).

- Impulsiveness + Flexibility joins Thoughtfulness + Integrity.

<u>Resource point – 4</u>

- Emotionally expressive at 4 when 1s are unable to control their feelings.

- Bottled up emotions, or emotions that were held back for long, now starts spilling out.

- Drawback: Stress and the overwhelming feeling might lead to a hurtful or riotous way of opening up.

- When the 1s move to 4, they get to know how they feel and what they need which works mostly in their favor.

Point 2 – The Giver

Wing Points

2s have two wings – 1 and 3.

Predominant 1 wing

- Natural trait of 2s gets balanced (with 1 wing) by the need to *get things right*.

- More controlled and organized.

- Tend to get thoughtful by balancing their emotional side with self-discipline and the need to analyze the situations.

- Drawback: Physical tension and inner conflict. 2s get uncomfortable if they have to be perfect all the time (which is the trait of wing 1).

- Advantage: 1s self-containment and 2s outgoing energy give an efficient and steady style.

Predominant 3 wing

- Meet the expectations of others to become professionally successful.

- Flexible, hard working and responsive.

- Drawback: Will have to slow down to avoid losing energy fast as 2s are not the real 3s. Will also face difficulty in bringing attention to their own feelings and needs.

- Advantage: Activeness of 3 wing can make 2s excellent performers and efficient communicators.

Dynamic Points

2s have two dynamic points – 4 (relaxation point) and 8 (resource point).

<u>Relaxation point – 4</u>

- More attentive to their inner self unlike the 2s usual style of paying more attention to others.

- Ability to feel their emotions and inner needs.

- 2s might get stuck in the melancholy or grief state similar to the 4s when they try to find *the missing factor*.

- Ability to know what they really want can help the 2s to develop the emotional intensity.

- Successful integration of the 2s with the 4s can help to balance the emotional and external connection. They can find a *home within their self*.

<u>Resource point – 8</u>

- Making this a productive position entirely depends on how the 2s manage the 8s (as they are quite the opposite).

- 2s usually go with the flow, while 8s take charge. Most 2s will have difficulty in moving to 8 and will do so only when there is a lot of external stress or pressure.

- If handled well, 2s can learn how to handle conflict from the 8s, as it doesn't come to the 2s naturally.

- 2s can also be able to set boundaries and develop the skill of saying *no* when they really want to.

Point 3 – The Performer

Wing Points

3s have two wings – 2 and 4.

<u>Predominant 2 wing</u>

- Tend to be engaging and warm.

- Ability to make a personal connection at work.

- Overall accomplishments will be accompanied by a successful relationship with the team.

- 3s usually have more people skills as they are more of an extrovert compared to the 2s.

- Drawback: Reinforcing dependency for external recognition and approval, which is common with both 2s and 3s, may lead to bad taste.

- Advantage: Influence of the 2 wing can help the 3s to get more skilled in managing and leading a large team.

Predominant 4 wing

- 3s have more access to their internal moods and emotions with the dominance of wing 4. This will encourage them to create their own personal agenda.

- May retreat from their busy work state to analyze their options and choices.

- Drawback: 3s can get into depression if they work too much on their personal feelings.

- Advantage: 2s, who are usually more into people orientation, can get influenced by wing 4 to focus on the intellectual content.

Dynamic Points

3s have two dynamic points – 6 (relaxation point) and 9 (resource point)

Relaxation point – 6

- 3s start to think about their relationships, desires and lives when they feel safe enough to take a break from their constant action.

- 3s with the 6 territory provide the ability to develop strategy, ask the right questions and understand the opposing forces that are basically necessary for long-term success. This works well for the ones who are in the leadership position.

- Instead of taking on goals and plans without rationale thinking, 3s at point 6 get motivated to make informed and logical decisions.

- Sometimes being at 6 can give 3s unusual experiences of doubt and fear, but these insecure or disturbed feelings are required as they confirm that they are working on their professional and personal development.

Resource point – 9

- Point 9 helps the 3s to develop the ability to see things from others' point of view and to bring people together on the task in an approachable fashion instead of being too directive or competitive which is the usual trait of 3.

- When 3s move into 9, they tend to slow down and listen to the rhythms of the body (to take rest when needed and get back to the active mode when ready).

- Stress and too much work can force the 3s to move into 9, leading them to become inert or static which is basically not their character.

- However, 3s can benefit from harmony and hold grounding qualities if they can move to 9 without much pressure or stress.

Point 4 – The Romantic

Wing Points

4s have two wings – 3 and 5.

Predominant 3 wing

- Turn their attention towards the world.

- Can be successful in business if the 4s work in synchronization with wing 3.

- 4s can blend in by putting aside too much of their individualism but, at the same time, leave their personalized touch in the presentation or style.

- 4s can meet the expectation of others, but there will be mild friction when it comes to balancing their inner world and social life as 4s are always *into their own inner world*.

- Drawback: 4s can get impatient with shallow or ordinary activities and will want to get into things that offer greater intensity. This may lead to a complaining mode, or it can push them to look for excellence in whatever they get their hands on.

Predominant 5 wing

- 4s tend to look for a lifestyle, which can offer a lot of privacy, or will look for jobs that give them enough time to turn their attention inwards. Example: Writers, scholars, artists and musicians will fit the band.

- 4s like to work in a workplace set-up, which will require minimum contact with others, although there is an inner feeling of being in a relationship with the others, but at a distance.

- Compared to the 4s with wing 3, 4s with wing 5 will not be too concerned about meeting their colleague's expectations or to the intricacy of interpersonal relationships.

- Drawback: They will be looked at as arrogant, weird or unfriendly people.

- Advantage: The creative skills of the 4s with wing 5 will make up for their lack of people skills.

Dynamic Points

4s have two dynamic points – 1 (relaxation point) and 2 (resource point).

<u>Relaxation point – 1</u>

- 4s become emotionally calm and physically grounded when they are appreciated and feel secure, as the gravitational center shifts to the belly center.

- Less moody and have fewer emotional swings.

- 4s moving to relaxation point 1 helps them to think practically with lower feelings of longing or gloominess.

- 4s start to stand up for self instead of feeling victimized. They get more stable with self-assertion and instinctual energy instead of impulsive, angry outbursts.

- 4s who are quick in criticizing others tend to look for improvement in others when they move to point 1, thereby making an effort to stay gracious and friendly.

Resource point – 2

- 4s on point 2 usually feel that they are stressing out self by staying nice for too long and will need to move forward for their own benefit.

- They also feel that they are losing their individuality by playing nice to gain personal connections and people's approval.

- However, if 4s are able to take it under control, point 2 can help them come out of their isolated state and connect with the outside world in a better way.

- 4s can try to choose this approach in a professional environment for a healthy work set-up, as being stuck in their own interior world might give assumptions to others.

Point 5 – The Observer

Wing Points

5s have two wings – 4 and 6.

<u>Predominant 4 wing</u>

- 5s with wing 4 have an active emotional life, which can influence their behavior and decision.

- Integrating the feeling and thinking center is the challenge here – they shouldn't create conflict or pull them in different directions.

- Drawback: Although wing 4 can support the 5s to develop better interpersonal warmth, it might also lead them to disorganized or unpredictable style.

- This wing helps the 4s to emphasize more on improving relationships instead of getting into materialistic or scientific models.

- Compassion is more important when it comes to relationships; therefore, most 5s tend to get pulled towards this wing when they are looking for a personal connection, especially with partners or romantic interests.

Predominant 6 wing

- 5s with wing 6 will try to reinforce their mental center by focusing on the technical data, information and knowledge when it comes to solving life's challenges.

- Drawback: 5s tend to feel increased worry and fear, thereby magnifying the dangers and threats than they actually are. They may try to get detached or put up more boundaries.

- Advantage: Wing 6 helps in reinforcing the incredible ability of being insightful, thus giving space for creativity, which is a natural trait of the 5. 5s are loyal to a relationship, similar to the 6s.

Dynamic Points

5s have two dynamic points – 8 (relaxation point) and 7 (resource point).

Relaxation point – 8

- The shift of 5s when they move to point 8 can be dramatic – the quiet withdrawn 5 will suddenly become more expressive, assertive and body-based. This shifting paradigm can be challenging for their partner or friend.

- Both point 5 and point 8 are always self-centric, i.e., he or she keeps referring only about self. Listening and hearing the other person's viewpoint is always difficult.

- 5s in point 8 can have a lot of good positive energy when appropriately managed.

- It is incredible if the detached 5 is able to feel the grounding of point 8.

- 5s who pass through the line regularly (point 8) when they are into physical activities such as martial arts, sports or other outdoor action.

<u>Resource point – 7</u>

- The reserved 5s become more extroverted and outgoing when they move to point 7.

- 5s in this point can act in two different ways – they can be the life of the party and spread their vibrant energy everywhere, or they can be pressurized when talking to people.

- 5s can feel stressful being at 7 at such situations and will want to recoil and retreat to their own private space.

Point 6 – The Loyal Skeptic

Wing Points

6s have two wings – 5 and 7.

Predominant 5 wing

- 6s with wing 5 will want to preserve their confidentiality and privacy for security purposes.

- May feel uncomfortable and aloof among people in social gatherings.

- Knowledge is valued more than experience and they will want to figure out things before springing into action.

- More emphasis is given to cognitive abilities.

- Drawback: Have the tendency to put off decisions or postpone things that need visibility.

- 6s with wing 5 prefer structured and methodical situations and therefore might work as scholars, professors, scientists, teachers or writers.

- Sense of security depends on the relationship they have with friends and family.

- They tend to keep all the agreements (paperwork) in place.

- At times, they feel isolated or have mixed feelings towards people.

Predominant 7 wing

- 6s with wing 7 can be pushed to participate in adventures and have an enjoyable experience.

- Like the 7, 6s get excited to create interesting plans, but it is crucial to know their limits as the 6s always have their skeptical mindset.

- They try to engage others when it comes to discussing issues or ideas.

- 6s with wing 7 can be comprehensive but be too criticizing, be sociable but edgy.

- *Agree to disagree* – most 6s with this wing go by this.

- Group projects, group trips and group sports are mostly preferred.

Dynamic Points

6s have two dynamic points – 9 (relaxation point) and 3 (resource point).

<u>Relaxation point – 9</u>

- The shift of 6s to point 9 can be noticed when they drop their center of gravity to the belly. They accept things as it happens and often are less concerned about figuring out things.

- 6s usually foresee problems and question the motives of people, and are cautious in dangerous situations, but, when they move to point 9, all of this withers away.

- Point 9 makes them more relaxed, but if the 6s exert too much, they can end up with inertia (the problems faced by the 9s).

- When done the right way, 6s with point 9 can have a combination of an instinctual grounded feeling and insightful intellect.

- Most 6s with point 9 work out or get into athletics to evade the *bigger perspective of the mind*. This way they don't need to relax their mind and therefore tend to go with the flow (the usual style of 9).

Resource point – 3

- 6s with point 3 get to achieve their results quickly as they get into action mode immediately.

- No excessive thinking or doubting their own self.

- Instead of getting controlled by the intellect or rules of point 3, the energy of point 3 acts more adjustable and approachable for the 6s. This is more about meeting the expectations of the external factors.

- When it comes to business, 6s are pushed or pulled to the point 3. 6s can manage it to a point, but it can get stressful for them so, to avoid falling sick, it is necessary to get back to their home base (point 6).

Point 7 – The Epicure

Wing Points

7s have two wings – 6 and 8.

Predominant 6 wing

- 7s with wing 6 become more of the mental-types – they tend to always be within their heads by not concentrating on their emotional and bodily feelings.

- They have the ability to envision, think, plan and execute things at incredible alertness and mental speed.

- 7s incorporate the loyalty (character) of wing 6 in them.

- Moving to this wing can make them more committed to relationships, and also display a good rapport and understanding within the teams in a professional environment.

Predominant 8 wing

- 7s with wing 8 get attracted to physical and sensate experiences, and will want more adventure in their life (travel, extreme sports, party, business ventures, etc.).

- When both the home base and dominant wing are in the expansive mode, they can get too far into the world – it would be difficult finding them at home or being stuck in a cubicle in the office.

- They believe they can do whatever they dream.

- Drawback: This over-excitement and self-referencing can lead them to lose their grounding.

- Advantage: This quality makes them extremely creative leading to self-absorption, but, if they are ready to take accountability for a venture or work for someone apart from self, they can expand more and feel the joy.

Dynamic Points

7s have two dynamic points – 5 (relaxation point) and 1 (resource point).

<u>Relaxation point – 5</u>

- 7s feel secure and safe when they move to point 5. They also tend to correct their over-reactive self.

- Moving to point 5 makes the 7s to withdraw within self by going deep and silent. They tend to encounter frustration and fright in the process.

- Drawback: They feel lonely or get bored too soon.

- Advantage: Most 7s understand that getting centered within self can provide clarity in thoughts and perception, and it is good to withdraw once in a while and silence the mind from the gushing flow of activity outside.

- Since this is not how 7s usually are, they quickly get back to their normal self when people around ask – *why are you so withdrawn and silent?* But, if they are able to work well with point 5, they tend to get stronger by centering self, setting limits and making smart choices.

Resource point – 1

- The shift that happens when the 7s move to point 1 can be intense.

- 7s usually don't expect too much from the environment, but the traits of point 1 are that everything needs to be perfect.

- Moving to 1 can make the 7s more judgmental, critical and angry as they get stressed when they are pushed to make things right always.

- They change from '*All ok*' to '*You are not doing it right.*'

- If they are able to handle the shift properly, they get to incorporate the structures of point 1. They tend to get more systematic, organized, focused, get to the action and always look for options.

Point 8 – The Protector

Wing Points

8s have two wings – 7 and 9.

Predominant 7 wing

- 8s with wing 7 become more gregarious, amiable and charismatic.

- Similar to the 7s with wing 8, 8s with wing 7 will love to experience adventures, but unlike the 7s, 8s tend to be more physically grounded.

- They get incredible access to enthusiasm, dynamism and energy.

- Channeling the energy well will help the 8s become successful in any field – be it athletes, entrepreneurs, warriors, contractors or artists.

- Drawback: Since both 8s and 7s are self-referencing, they tend to always look out for self, rather than being considerate to others.

- Hearing the impact of their behavior on others can make them change.

Predominant 9 wing

- Wing 9 makes the 8s more laid back, making their energy levels a bit quieter.

- Instead of leading, they tend to work or exercise control from behind the scenes.

- 8s with wing 9 become obsessive as their aggressive quality gets bottled up inside and they get stuck with repeated behavioral patterns.

- Like the 9s, the 8s with this wing face trouble in getting things started, have low momentum and difficulty in changing directions.

- Drawback: The 8s with this wing start getting angry to get things moving and to escape from stillness.

Dynamic Points

8s have two dynamic points – 2 (relaxation point) and 5 (resource point).

<u>Relaxation point – 2</u>

- 8s get closer to their emotional center when they move to point 2.

- The usual caring and generous 8s tend to become open or vulnerable. In general, 8s keep their defenses and boldness strong to face a world filled with inconsistency and moving to point 2 can bring their tender and vulnerable side.

- It takes a lot of courage for them to open up.

- 8s in point 2 spend more time in the heart point, making them more gentle and caring (which the 2s are good at).

- They offer a different kind of intelligence while taking decisions, and tend to come out with positive energy.

Resource point – 5

- 8s who look for privacy almost regularly move to point 5, as even the 5s need their own space.

- 8s who usually take charge of situations tend to become quieter when in 5, allowing them to reflect on their thoughts and strategize accordingly.

- Since 8s are always into everything, moving to 5 can help them to detach and distance for some time.

- If not handled properly, 8s staying in point 5 for long can lead to depression as they tend to shut down completely.

Point 9 – The Mediator

Wing Points

9s have two wings – 8 and 1.

Predominant 8 wing

- 9s with wing 8 tend to show their angry, rebellious side, as 8s are usually more of a rebel.

- 9s get more assertive, but when managed well it helps them in their professional environment, especially in the leadership area.

- They willingly come forward to fight for justice and truth either the 9s way or the 8s way (angry explosion).

Predominant 1 wing

- 9s in wing 1 get perfect, organized, principled and methodical. The wing 1 can pull the 9s into their territory, such that it becomes almost impossible to differentiate the personality of a 9 from the 1.

- 9s take control of the situation, but try to get things done in harmony – be good, follow the rules and everything will fall into place.

- The usual rebellious 9s are compelled to abide by the expectations of *the influential figures (authority)* with wing 1 taking dominance.

- Being the actual 9, they often overcome the 1s role and show passive aggression by moving away or forgetting.

Dynamic Points

9s have two dynamic points – 3 (relaxation point) and 6 (resource point).

Relaxation point – 3

- 9s become more active in the feeling center, but at times it can get too overwhelming for them.

- 9s in point 3 are able to maintain a good connection in a relationship as unlike the usual way of 9s where they wait, think, sit on it before communicating, 9s in point 3 pushes them to decide faster.

Resource point – 6

- 9s who get motivated or pressurized by external events or face conflicts when they got to step out of their comfort zone, they move to point 6.

- 9s in point 6 can focus on the trouble spots instead of looking only at the issue that is disturbing them.

- Moving to point 6 helps them to differentiate between the various options and chart their action plan.

- Drawback: 9s in point 6 can get more fearful or anxious and sometimes are not familiar when it comes to handling critical situations.

Chapter Six:
Different options

Enneagram can be used as a therapeutic and a diagnostic aid to work on personal growth and development. When you accept your basic personality and dominant wing, you indirectly acknowledge the necessity to work on the underdeveloped areas. Integrating and incorporating the positives of a particular point (resource point or relaxation point) can help you grow better as a person. This is the natural and organic way of developing self.

How do you grow?

When you consciously implement the following by questioning self and start your quest for a better awakening, you create a win-win situation for self and for the others around you.

- Work on developing the underdeveloped wing (the less dominant wing). Although both your wings are active, one wing is more predominant compared to the other wing. You will need to work towards developing the *shadow persona* of self.

- You usually get fixated to a primary center (Thinking, Feeling, Instinctual (doing) centers), but try going counter-clockwise to the next center and develop that particular center within you.

- Try getting into the meditative state every day – this allows you to detach yourself from the habitual way of thinking. When you get into this non-thinking state and hold it for at least a few seconds, you will be able to grow the ability of detaching yourself from your normal life. A form of grounding! This allows you to observe your own self and find out *what you need from life.* You get into a calm and peaceful state of mind.

- When you are able to detach yourself, you can slowly develop your ability to shift your focus to the remaining 8 Enneagram types you inherently have but, again, don't overexert. Spend less time in the other 8 types. When you are successful in doing this, you tend to be more flexible and get the ability to make wise choices.

- Each Enneagram type has its own unique way of being present *in the moment,* i.e., mindfulness. Working on your type helps you grow!

Examples:

Enneagram Types	Mindfulness
Type 1	Attempting to achieve accuracy in work, environment and self.

Type 2	Serving and caring for others.
Type 3	Performing a role efficiently that leads to visible achievement.
Type 4	Exploring own individuality and distinguishing self from others.
Type 5	Observing any object of attention by getting into detached mode.
Type 6	Apprehending potential problems or dangers.
Type 7	Looking for experiences, possibilities and potential pleasures in the environment.
Type 8	Attempting to take control and achieve dominance over the environment.
Type 9	Bringing harmony to self, others and the environment

In this case, the environment can be external as well as internal. Exercising mindfulness will require one to lose self in the mindsets to achieve inner tranquility. It is not easy to practice mindfulness techniques as it takes a lot of practice.

Spending a few seconds in meditation can help you overcome the hurdles you experience.

Sit down and focus on your breath – every single breath. Concentrate on your breath as you inhale and exhale. Let your mind be empty of thoughts. Your breathing should be your only focus.

It may be difficult initially, but with regular practice, you will gradually be able to gain momentum in your life.

You can try the following to achieve mindfulness depending on your Enneagram type:

Enneagram Types	How to work?
Type 1	Let go! Experience how it feels when you let go of your grudges, pain and negative emotions.
Type 2	Spend time with self. Look into you!
Type 3	Live the moment. Realize the importance of *being present*.
Type 4	Stay grounded. Feel it!
Type 5	Go for direct experiences. Realize the insight behind it.

Type 6	Feel your *feeling center*. Experience the comfort of you!
Type 7	Experience joy in the smallest things. Make the ordinary feel extraordinary!
Type 8	Feel how strong it is when you are not in control! Loosen up!
Type 9	Seek the harmony within you!

It is important to understand the blockage you face from within, acknowledge it, accept the barrier and then tell yourself you can do it despite the entire barrier. Don't be judgmental always! You do *push-ups* to strengthen your body, so, similarly, *meditate* to strengthen your mind. Anchor the ship by being its captain!

Conclusion

We have come to the end of this book. I would like to take this opportunity to thank you once again for choosing this book.

The book has covered the primary objective, which is to serve as a guide to help you identify your strengths and weaknesses based on your Enneagram types. The chapters take you on tour to all the nine Enneagram types, its nine points and three centers. They also focus on the positives and negatives of the type when they move into a particular wing point or dynamic point. It gives a quick brief on how to accept, acknowledge and work towards your personal growth.

I sincerely hope this book was useful and has helped in answering most of the queries you had in mind.

Thank you and best wishes!

One last thing

If you enjoyed this book, would you please take a minute and post an honest review of it on Amazon? I'd really appreciate it, as it will help me get these ideas out there to more people!

Thank you.

And if you forget to check the Enneagram Test I'm giving along with this book as a gift, you can get it here: Download the Enneagram Test by visiting this link:

http://eepurl.com/dtlgxf

About the Author

When we were young, no one told Eleanor she need not understand life to live it fully, and I think she wouldn't believe it if they'd have done so. Since our childhood, she was always the quiet girl who saw the world in her unique perspective. Back then, the other kids saw her different, at least at first, but I always saw her as the wisest person I knew.

Her love story with Enneagram started during her work at the university. At first, she got into learning about Enneagram to have a better understanding of the people she deals with daily, but soon she looked inward. That was a turning point in her life.

After several years of feeling different, and getting more and more distant from others because of her way of thinking and her emotional distance, she suddenly had the gift of realization that nothing is wrong with her. She recognized that both the things she loved about herself and the things she felt different about, belong to the Observers, the Type 5s.

From then, she saw her uniqueness as a gift; she learnt to accept herself and live her life fulfilled as a Type 5 (which now she's proud of). Enneagram became a journey to understand herself and find her bliss and a mission to help others live their lives fully.

-   Elliott Cooper

Made in the USA
San Bernardino, CA
04 January 2019